Start with Art

Animals

© Aladdin Books Ltd 1999

Designed and produced by
Aladdin Books Ltd
28 Percy Street
London W1P 0LD

First published in the United States in 1999 by
Copper Beech Books,
an imprint of
The Millbrook Press
2 Old New Milford Road
Brookfield, Connecticut 06804

Project Editor
Sally Hewitt

Editor
Liz White

Design
David West Children's Book Design

Designer
Flick Killerby

Illustrator
Rob Shone

Picture Research
Carlotta Cooper/Brooks Krikler Research

Printed in Belgium
All rights reserved

Cataloging-in-Publication Data is on file at the Library of Congress

ISBN 0-7613-3263-4 (lib.bdg.)
ISBN 0-7613-0828-8 (pbk)

The project editor, Sally Hewitt, is an experienced teacher. She writes and edits books for children on a wide variety of subjects including art, music, science and math.

The author, Sue Lacey, is an experienced teacher of art. She currently teaches elementary school children in England. In her spare time, she paints and sculpts.

photocredits: Abbreviations: t-top, m-middle, b-bottom, r-right, l-left, c-center
All the pictures in this book are by Vanessa Bailey apart from the following pages: Cover b, 8b, 11, 15, 31: AKG/Erich Lessing; 4b, 21, 23: AKG London; 13: AKG. © Succession Picasso/DACS 1999; 17: Frank Spooner Pictures; 19: Reproduced by Permission of the Henry Moore Foundation; 25: AKG. © DACS 1999; 27: James Davis Travel Photography; 28b: Tate Gallery Publications. © Estate of Gwen John 1999. All rights reserved, DACS.

Start with Art

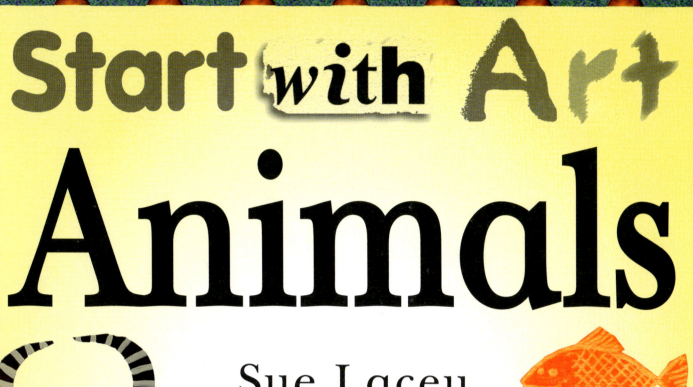

Animals

Sue Lacey

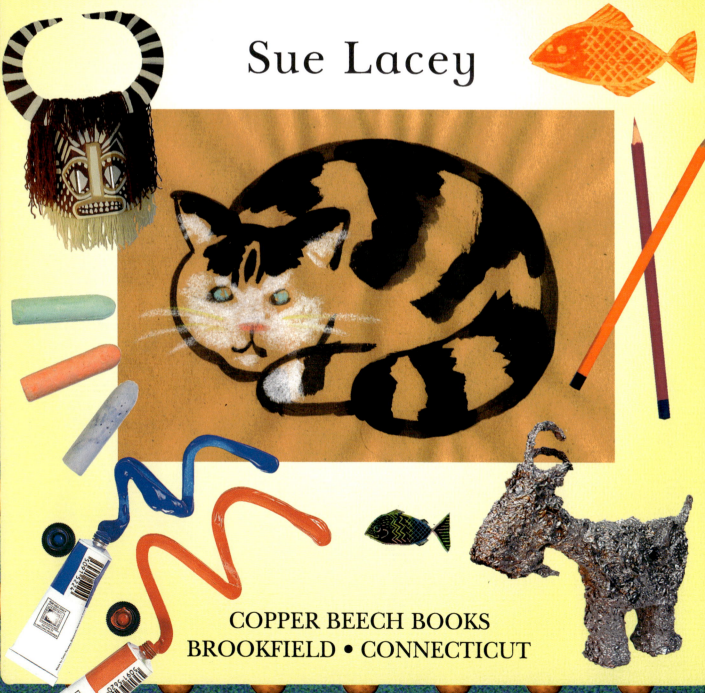

COPPER BEECH BOOKS
BROOKFIELD • CONNECTICUT

INTRODUCTION

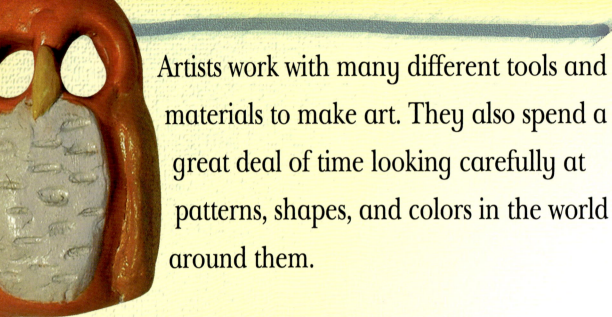

Artists work with many different tools and materials to make art. They also spend a great deal of time looking carefully at patterns, shapes, and colors in the world around them.

This book is about how artists see **animals**. On every page you will find a work of art by a different famous artist, which will give you ideas and inspiration for the project.

You don't have to be a brilliant artist to do the projects. Look at each piece of art, learn about the artist, and have fun being creative.

CONTENTS

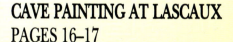

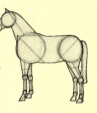

WORKING LIKE AN ARTIST

It can help you in your work if you start by looking carefully and collecting ideas, just like an artist. Artists usually carry a sketchbook around with them so they can get their ideas on paper right away.

Words
You can write some words to remind you of the shapes, colors, and patterns you see.

Materials
Try out different pencils, pens, paints, pastels, crayons, and materials to see what they do. Which would be the best for this work?

Color
When using color, mix all the colors you want first and try them out. It is amazing how many different colors you can make.

Using a sketchbook Before you start each project, this is the place to do your sketches. Try out your tools and materials, mix colors, and stick in some interesting papers and fabrics. You can then choose which you want to use.

Be a magpie

Make a collection of things that you find interesting, like feathers, stones, or materials. Anything that catches your eye could be useful in your artwork.

Art box You can collect tools and materials for your work and put them in a box. Sometimes you may need to go to an art shop to buy exactly what you need. Often you can find things at home you can use. Ask for something for your art box for your birthday!

Drawing animals

It may seem difficult to draw animals, but if you take your time, do some sketches, and observe carefully, you can do it!

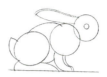

Body shapes
Start by drawing simple shapes to show the head, body, legs, tail, and ears.

Proportion
Make sure you have made the head the right size, and check that the legs are not too long or too short.

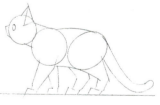

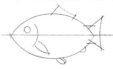

Fur, hair, and skin
Does the animal have fur, hair, skin, or unusual colors? Find out how you will draw them by trying out some ideas in your sketchbook.

Finishing touches
Once you have the size and shapes right, you can start to fill in the details and add color.

REALISTIC DRAWING

WHAT YOU NEED
Pencil • Paper
Ruler • Compass
Colored Pencils

Horses were George Stubbs's favorite animals. He studied them for ten years, doing hundreds of drawings of them. He made these into a book that artists and veterinarians used in their work. You can practice drawing a horse by using simple geometric shapes.

GALLERY

Horse and Rider 1771
GEORGE STUBBS (1724 – 1806)

CONTRAST
A careful use of light and dark shades of color bring the horse to life. Stubbs made the horse darker than his master so you look at the horse first.

REALISTIC
Look at the horse's muscles. They look so real that the painting could almost be a photograph.

George Stubbs was born in Liverpool, England. He taught himself to draw, paint, and make etchings. He spent years studying horses and became a famous horse painter. Rich people paid him to paint them in their huge grounds, by their big houses, with their favorite horses.

PROJECT: DRAWING

Step 1. Look carefully at Stubbs's horse. Draw a square with two diagonal lines crossing it. Draw a large circle in the top left corner and a small one in the top right.

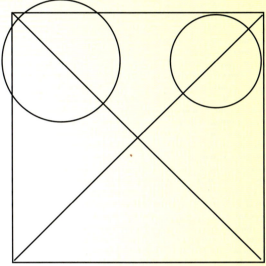

Step 2. Now add some straight lines from the circles for legs. Put small circles for the knee and ankle joints. The head and neck can be added by using straight lines and a large and small circle.

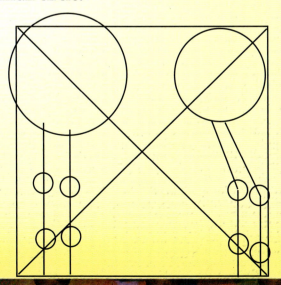

Step 3. You can finish the drawing by adding the body, neck, ears, legs, and tail to the lines and circles. When you have practiced drawing a few horses you can add color to them.

ROMAN MOSAIC

WHAT YOU NEED
Cardboard • Pencil
Picture to Copy
Selection of Beans
and Lentils
Craft Glue

Mosaics were used by the Romans to decorate walls, floors, and pavements. This dog was found in Pompeii, Italy. It is a warning sign saying, "Beware of the Dog." Why not make your own mosaic of your pet or any interesting animal?

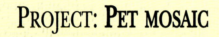

PROJECT: PET MOSAIC

Step 1. Draw a simple outline of your animal on cardboard. Use a photograph or picture from a magazine or book to help you.

Step 2. Collect dried beans, lentils, and other peas of different colors. Spread craft glue onto the cardboard and stick them on to make your animal.

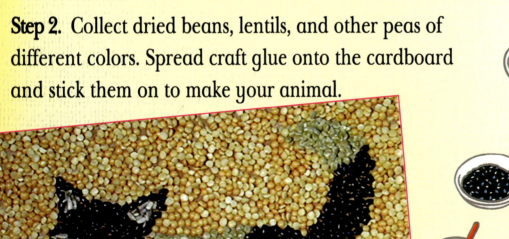

GALLERY

Beware of the Dog AD 79
POMPEII MOSAIC

MATERIALS
Mosaics were usually made from many small, colored stones, tiles, or marble. This one was made from marble pieces.

WARNING
The dog looks as fierce as the artist could make it, to scare people away.

COLORS
Marble is never found in very bright colors, so the tones used for this dog are natural: red, white, and gray.

DECORATION
Mosaics were used to decorate palaces and churches in ancient times.

This mosaic was discovered in the remains of Pompeii long after Mount Vesuvius had erupted in AD 79. It was probably made to lie in the sidewalk outside a wealthy person's house. It would have acted as a warning to passersby to beware of the dog; it would also warn thieves to keep away!

ASSEMBLAGE

WHAT YOU NEED
Craft Glue • Foil
Tape • Scissors
Cardboard • Knife
Ruler

Picasso used different materials he may have found in his workshop or yard to make his goat. Look around your home for cardboard, tape, and foil to make a three–dimensional model like this.

PROJECT: 3–D MODEL

Step 1. Cut an oval shape out of cardboard. Draw two lines across the center with a knife and ruler (this is called scoring; ask an adult to help). Fold along the lines.

Step 2. Cut three rectangles out of cardboard. Score three lines on each and fold to make the neck and two pairs of legs. Copy the shape on the left, score along the lines, and fold for the head.

Step 3. Use lots of tape to join all of the pieces together. Cut the bottoms of the legs and fold outward to help the model stand.

Step 4. Ears and horns can be cut out from the leftover cardboard. Bend the horns into a curve and tape them onto the goat's head.

Step 5. Finish by gluing scrunched-up aluminum foil all around the goat and adding a tail and beard.

GALLERY

Goat 1950
PABLO PICASSO (1881 – 1973)

MATERIALS
Picasso used plaster, wood, and clay to make his goat. How many different textures can you see in the sculpture?

WOOD
The goat is standing on an old piece of wood. Other pieces of wood have been used to make the surface of the animal look more interesting.

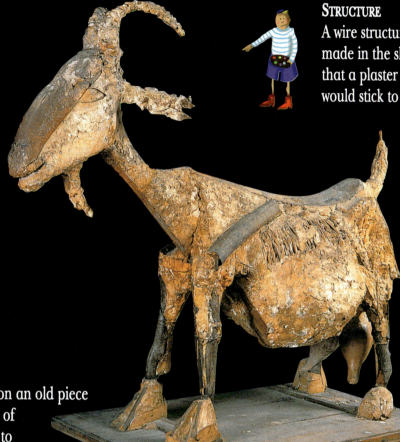

STRUCTURE
A wire structure would have been made in the shape of a goat so that a plaster of Paris mixture would stick to it.

POSE
Can you see the goat is looking up with a perky tail and ears? How would you describe Picasso's goat?

Through his paintings, sculpture, drawings, and ceramics, the Spanish artist Pablo Picasso changed how people saw art in the twentieth century. He used many different kinds of materials to create his works of art. He was always making something unusual, right to the end of his life. Sometimes he would make sculpture by using bits and pieces he found. This is how he made this lively goat.

ATTENTION TO DETAIL

WHAT YOU NEED
Paint • Pencil
Orange Stick
Printing Block
Clay / Play Dough
Paper

Dürer has drawn his hare in great detail, looking carefully at the fur, eyes, ears, and nose. You can make a print of your own pet using Dürer's hare to help you. Try to put in as many details as you can.

PROJECT: ANIMAL PRINT

Step 1. Make a sketch of your pet using a pencil and paper. Put in as many small details as you can. Look carefully at the fur, face, and tail.

Step 2. Use a sharp pencil or orange stick to draw your pet onto a printing block. You can use flattened-out clay or play dough instead.

Step 3. Cover the printing block with paint. Try out the print on a scrap of paper first. Press it firmly down onto the paper and rub over the back of it. Pull it away carefully. When you are pleased with it you can print onto your best paper.

GALLERY

Young Hare 1502
ALBRECHT DÜRER (1471 – 1528)

DETAIL
A very fine brush was used to put in all the small details. You can see almost every hair and whisker on the hare.

FEATURES
Can you see how realistic this hare is? The nails look very sharp, the eyes bright, and the ears listening.

PAINTING
Dürer usually made prints. He probably did this painting in his spare time for pleasure.

MOVEMENT
Although the hare is sitting still, Dürer has made it look very alert, as if it will leap off at any minute.

Albrecht Dürer was born in Germany and trained to be a goldsmith with his father. He soon got bored and went off traveling. In Italy, he found he enjoyed drawing, printing, and painting, and he quickly became famous for his book illustrations. He loved showing every small detail in his work. He did this with his prints as well as his paintings.

CAVE ART

WHAT YOU NEED
Oil Pastels /
Charcoal Pencil
Sketchbook
Pencil • Thick
Cardboard • Acrylic
Paints
Sand

Long ago, people painted the walls of caves with pictures of animals and sometimes people. The paintings were probably thought of as magic and were painted in special places away from where people lived.

PROJECT: WALL DRAWING

Step 1. Find a piece of thick cardboard. Mix some sand with white and pale yellow acrylic paint. Cover the cardboard with the paint to make it look like the wall of a cave.

Step 2. Sketch some outlines of animals in your sketchbook. Copy two or three onto your homemade wall, using a black oil pastel or charcoal pencil.

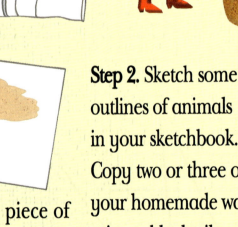

Step 3. Shade each animal with yellow and reddish brown, which were the colors used by cave artists.

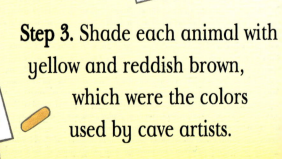

GALLERY

Horse 17,000 BC
LASCAUX CAVE PAINTING

SURFACE
You can see that this horse has been drawn on a wall by looking carefully at the surface. Can you see the cracks, scratches, and marks there?

LINE
It is easy to see the outline of this horse even though it is very old. The artist would have used a sharpened stick dipped in dark earth.

EYE
Which way do you think this horse is looking? Perhaps it is wondering what will be coming up behind it.

MAGIC
Ancient people were often afraid of things they did not understand. They thought their paintings made a magic that would help them.

This horse is part of a 100-foot-long gallery of prehistoric cave paintings at Lascaux in France. The only colors used were made from powdered rock and soil. White, green, and blue were not used because they could not be made. The paintings were often made in dark caves, and this helped to protect them so that we can still see them today.

CLAY SCULPTURE

WHAT YOU NEED
Clay • Paints
Brushes
Craft Glue
Plastic Knife

Henry Moore's owl is a very simple shape, but you couldn't mistake it for any other animal or bird. He started making his owl in plaster and finished it in bronze. You can make an owl by molding clay and using simple shapes and textures.

PROJECT: CLAY OWL

Step 1. Soften some clay in your hands and form it into an owl shape. Push two holes through the clay for its eyes by using your finger or a plastic knife.

Step 2. You can add wings, a beak, and feet. Use different tools to make a rough texture on the clay like feathers.

Step 3. When the clay is dry, paint the owl and cover it with watered-down craft glue to varnish and protect it.

GALLERY

Owl 1966
HENRY MOORE (1898 – 1986)

SHAPE
The shape of this owl is very simple and there are few details, but you can still tell it is an owl.

HOLES
This owl has holes for eyes. Henry Moore often used holes in his sculptures to create interesting shapes and spaces.

TEXTURE
Can you see different marks on the surface of the owl? Do they make you think of feathers, a beak, and feet?

OBSERVATION
Before he started on his final sculpture, Henry Moore made many sketches and smaller plaster models.

Henry Moore was still working until he was almost ninety. He lived in England all his life. His huge sculptures of people, animals, and shapes can be seen in the countryside and many different cities all over the world. This owl is one of his smaller pieces and shows his careful observation, skill, and love of wildlife.

WHAT YOU NEED
Craft Glue • Pencil
Paints • Paint Brush
White Cardboard
Paper

EXPRESSIONISM

It was important to Franz Marc that he paint animals and their world as if he were looking through their eyes. He used colors that expressed a feeling rather than being exactly like the animal or landscape. A print can do this, too.

PROJECT: HORSE PRINTS

Step 1. Make some green, blue, red, and yellow watery paints. Use a thick brush and spread the different colors over a piece of white cardboard.

Step 2. Draw an outline of your favorite animal. If you choose to do a horse use Marc's picture to help you.

Step 3. Draw over the outline with craft glue using a container with a nozzle. Leave the glue to dry.

GALLERY

Blue Horse 1 1911
FRANZ MARC (1880 – 1916)

COLOR

Marc used colors in his paintings that did not clash but made the picture feel calm. He painted the world through the eyes of an animal. Here you see how Marc thought a horse saw the world it lived in.

BRUSH STROKES

You can see that Marc used sweeping brush strokes to paint the landscape and the horse's body.

COMPARISON

Compare how Marc and Stubbs (see page 8–9) painted their horses. Which one is more realistic, and which is more expressive?

The best paintings of Franz Marc's were done toward the end of his life. He thought each color had a mood of its own, and he wanted the color to draw people into the feelings in his painting. He was not interested in painting a realistic picture like Stubbs.

Step 4. Paint over the glue outline with dark paint. Press it onto a piece of spare paper to test it first. When you are ready, print one or two animals onto the cardboard you painted earlier.

JUNGLE PAINTING

Rousseau liked to paint animals in jungles with large leaves and colorful flowers. You can put a tiger in a jungle by cutting shapes out of scrap magazines and hiding the tiger behind them.

PROJECT: TIGER COLLAGE

Step 2. Collect gold, green, and brown colors from magazines. Cut out leaf and tree shapes. You can make some colorful flowers, too.

Step 1. Draw a tiger and color it with chalk pastels. Cut it out.

Step 3. Put the tiger onto a dark background and arrange the leaf, tree, and flower shapes around and on top of the tiger. Make sure you can still see it!

Step 4. Glue the shapes on when you like the arrangement. You have made a jungle collage.

GALLERY

Exotic Landscape With Tiger 1907
HENRI ROUSSEAU (1844 – 1910)

LEAVES
How many different leaf shapes can you see? Rousseau studied tropical plants in Paris so he could paint them.

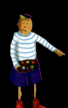

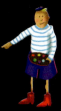

COLOR
The main color used by Rousseau is green. What effect does this have on the other colors he has used?

CAMOUFLAGE
Is it easy or difficult to see the tiger among the leaves? What is the tiger hiding from?

ANIMALS
There are two other animals watching and waiting to see what will happen. Can you see them?

When he retired from an office job, Henri Rousseau began to paint. He taught himself, and to his surprise soon became famous. Picasso liked his paintings and gave Rousseau a big party to celebrate his work. For this jungle painting, Henri Rousseau went to a zoo in Paris to study the tigers.

UNDERWATER DREAM

In his Fish Magic picture, Paul Klee used a mixture of paints to get the effect he wanted. His fish have interesting faces and skin patterns. They look as if they are hanging on strings, like a mobile. It is easy to make fish like Klee's.

PROJECT: FISH MOBILE

Step 1. Color a pattern onto two pieces of cardboard using bright crayons. Don't worry if the colors go on top of each other.

Step 2. Color over both patterns with black crayon. Use a fine stick to scratch out five or six fish shapes just through the black. Put patterns on each fish.

Step 3. Cut them out, tape a piece of thread onto the back. Glue them onto the other piece of cardboard facing back to back.

Step 4. Cut them out and scratch a pattern onto the back of each fish. Tie the fish onto two sticks or straws, leaving an end for hanging your mobile.

GALLERY

Fish Magic 1925
PAUL KLEE (1879 – 1940)

TIME
This fish tank has a sense of timelessness, yet in the center is a clock. It has stopped at the exact moment Paul Klee finished this painting.

DREAM
Klee wanted this painting to look like a dream while also seeming like a fish tank.

COLOR
The colors Klee has chosen to use are similar to those you might see at the bottom of a lake or the ocean.

STRANGE OBJECTS
A moon, a clown, and a vase are floating in this picture. What else can you see that is unusual?

Most of the important art galleries of the world have some of Paul Klee's paintings. He was born in Switzerland, but did most of his work in Germany. He liked to use his imagination and created many pictures that had a dreamlike feel to them, like this one. He used color, patterns, and shapes to express his ideas.

AFRICAN ANIMAL MASK

WHAT YOU NEED
String • Scissors
Cardboard • Pencils
Craft Glue • Paints
Brushes • Yarn

Many African masks are worn on special occasions. They are often used as part of a costume to tell a story about the tribe's history. Masks are great fun to make and wear, and can be made quite easily.

PROJECT: ANIMAL MASK

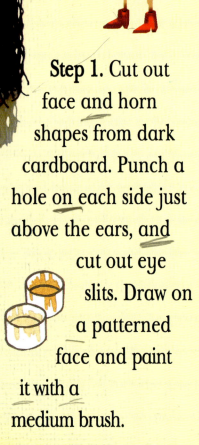

Step 1. Cut out face and horn shapes from dark cardboard. Punch a hole on each side just above the ears, and cut out eye slits. Draw on a patterned face and paint it with a medium brush.

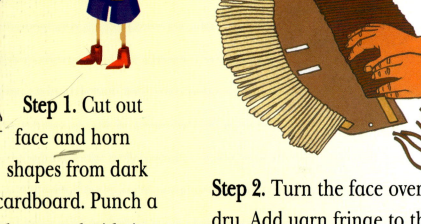

Step 2. Turn the face over when it i dry. Add yarn fringe to the bottom and cardboard strips to the top.

Step 3. Stick the horns on the front of the mask. Fold the cardboard over the horns like a fringe. Tie string through the holes and fasten over your face.

GALLERY

Shangaan Dancer in Costume (Present day)
VICTORIA FALLS, ZIMBABWE

PATTERN
Triangular lines over the eyes make the face look angry or fierce.

ANIMAL
What animal do you think this mask is supposed to be? What makes you think this?

FEELINGS
Masks were made to make people watching feel sad, frightened, or happy. How does this mask make you feel?

COLOR
Only brown, white, and black are used on this mask. It helps to make it look more dramatic.

African masks are made out of many different materials and are used for ceremonies such as weddings, funerals, or harvest. Sometimes wood is used, and feathers, straw, and paint are added as decoration. This mask is an animal with horns, and may be part of a hunting story.

OBSERVATIONAL DRAWING

WHAT YOU NEED
Inks • Pen
Brush • Pencil
Chalks • Cardboard
Sketchbook

Gwen John did many paintings of cats, and enjoyed using brush and ink with some white chalk highlights. Inks come in many different colors and can be used with brushes, pens, or a stick. Draw a portrait of your favorite cat. Use chalks to add color and give the cat some features.

GALLERY

Cat 1904–08
GWEN JOHN (1876 – 1939)

DETAIL
Just a few brush strokes and chalk marks make this little sleeping cat come to life.

BACKGROUND
Gwen John has used the brown color of the paper to play an important part in her drawing of her cat. Choice of surface can make all the difference in a work of art.

PROJECT: INK AND CHALK CAT

Step 1. Sketch your chosen cat standing, asleep, and walking. Choose your favorite pose and draw an outline of it on colored cardboard or paper.

Paris was the city Gwen John chose to live in after she had finished her art training in London. She wanted to get away from her father and her famous artist brother, Augustus. As she grew older she spent her life quietly, doing beautiful pale drawings and paintings of people, her cat, and parts of her house. She did not look after herself very well, and died of starvation when she was 63.

Step 2. Choose an ink that matches your cat, and go over your outline with pen or brush. You can water the ink down to make it lighter. Add details of pattern in the fur and markings on the face and tail. When it is dry, use colored chalks to add details like eyes, nose, whiskers, and colors in the fur.

IMAGINATION

WHAT YOU NEED
Scissors • Brush
Cardboard
Acrylic Paint
Pencils • Chalk
Any Interesting
Bright Things
Craft Glue

Raphael's painting tells the story of St. George fighting the dragon. Raphael used his imagination to make his dragon. He has made it look very wicked and dark. You can make a mixed media dragon that looks lively and colorful.

PROJECT: **MIXED MEDIA DRAGON**

Step 2. Paint in the patterns and shapes on the dragon's skin, wings, and face. Paint a bright color around the outline of the whole dragon.

Step 3. Cut up some silver, gold, and shiny paper and stick it onto the dragon. Sequins, buttons, shiny wrapping paper, and thread can be added, until you have a very bold dragon.

Step 1. Draw the outline of an imaginary dragon on dark cardboard with a light chalk or pencil line.

GALLERY

St. George Fighting With The Dragon c.1505
RAPHAEL (1483 – 1520)

DISTANCE
The dragon and St. George stand out, while the background fades into the distance in pale blues and greens.

DRAGON
Raphael used different tones of black and white to make the dragon's skin shine and gleam in an evil way.

WOMAN
St. George has rescued this woman from the evil dragon. Can you see how Raphael has made her look soft and delicate?

HORSE
Why do you think the horse is white? It certainly stands out in the center of the painting.

When Raphael was eleven, his father died. He then went to work in a studio to learn to become a painter. He became one of Italy's most famous artists. Best of all, he liked to paint the Holy Family and saints. In this painting he is showing how good overcomes evil, from the popular story of St. George saving the young woman from the terrors of the dragon.

GLOSSARY

CHARCOAL Slightly burned twigs or sticks that turn black and are used by artists for drawing.

ETCHING Acid is used to cut out a picture into a piece of metal. Ink is then put on and a print made of it.

EXPRESSIONISM A style of art that uses color, line, and shape to show emotion rather than to make pictures that look like the real world.

HIGHLIGHT Part of a painting or drawing that has been made lighter to show where the light is reflected.

MIXED MEDIA Many different kinds of materials used by artists to create unusual works of art.

MODEL A smaller than life, three-dimensional sculpture of an animal, person, or object.

MOLDING To change the shape of a material, like clay, into a new, more imaginative shape.

MOSAIC A picture or pattern made by arranging colored pieces of glass, marble, or stone.

OBSERVATION To look closely at something so that a more accurate work of art can be made.

REALISTIC A work of art that is made to look exactly like the real world.

SURFACE The outside of something that you can see and feel.

TEXTURE The feel or look of the outside or surface of something.

THREE-DIMENSIONAL An object or work of art that you can walk all around and look at from all sides.

TONES The many different shades or tints of a color.

INDEX